DICTIONARY OF

PREFIXES AND

SUFFIXES

USEFUL ENGLISH

AFFIXES

MANIK JOSHI

<u>Dedication</u>

THIS BOOK IS

DEDICATED

TO THOSE

WHO REALIZE

THE POWER OF ENGLISH

AND WANT TO

LEARN IT

SINCERELY

Copyright Notice

****

IMPORTANT NOTE

This Book is Part of a Series
SERIES Name: "English Word Power"
[A Twenty-Book Series]
BOOK Number: 05
BOOK Title: "Dictionary of Prefixes and Suffixes"
****

Table of Contents

DICTIONARY OF PREFIXES AND SUFFIXES..........................1

Dedication...2

Copyright Notice 3

Affixes, Prefixes and Suffixes.............................5

Prefixes and Suffixes -- A...................................6

Prefixes and Suffixes -- B.................................16

Prefixes and Suffixes -- C.................................17

Prefixes and Suffixes -- D.................................19

Prefixes and Suffixes -- E.................................24

Prefixes and Suffixes -- F.................................33

Prefixes and Suffixes -- G.................................34

Prefixes and Suffixes -- H.................................35

Prefixes and Suffixes -- I 37

Prefixes and Suffixes -- J 53

Prefixes and Suffixes -- K.................................54

Prefixes and Suffixes -- L 55

Prefixes and Suffixes -- M 61

Prefixes and Suffixes -- N.................................63

Prefixes and Suffixes -- O.................................67

Prefixes and Suffixes -- P and Q.........................71

Prefixes and Suffixes -- R.................................73

Prefixes and Suffixes -- S 75

Prefixes and Suffixes -- T 78

Prefixes and Suffixes -- U.................................79

Prefixes and Suffixes -- V.................................84

Prefixes and Suffixes -- W.................................85

Prefixes and Suffixes -- XYZ.............................86

About the Author..88

BIBLIOGRAPHY 89

Affixes, Prefixes and Suffixes

AFFIX

A letter or group of letters added to the **_beginning_** or **_end_** of a word to get a new word with a changed meaning.

Examples –

im- in **im**possible; **inter-** in **inter**national

-able in agree**able**; **-er** in learn**er**

English Affixes could be divided into two groups: Prefixes and Suffixes

PREFIX

A letter or group of letters added to the **_beginning_** of a word to get a new word with a changed meaning.

Examples –

im- in **im**possible; **inter-** in **inter**national; **un-** in **un**affected

SUFFIX

A letter or group of letters added to the **_end_** of a word to get a new word with a changed meaning.

Examples –

-able in agree**able**; **-er** in learn**er**; **-ness** in quick**ness**

Prefixes and Suffixes -- A

ENGLISH PREFIXES – A

a-

Used to form: adjectives, adverbs and nouns

General meaning: not, without

Examples:

acellular / **a**moral / **a**political / **a**theism / **a**theist / **a**typical

******

ad-

Used to form: nouns and verbs

General meaning: addition, tendency

Examples:

adjoin / **ad**judge / **ad**mixture

******

ambi-

Used to form: adjectives, adverbs and nouns

General meaning: both of two

Examples:

ambidexterity / **ambi**dextrous / **ambi**valence / **ambi**valent

******

ante-

Used to form: adjectives, nouns and verbs

General meaning: prior to; in front of

Examples:

antedate / **ante**natal / **ante**rior / **ante**-room

******

anti-

Used to form: adjectives and nouns

General meaning: against; the opposite of; preventing

Examples:

anti-aircraft / **anti**-bacterial / **anti**biotic / **anti**body / **anti**-choice / **anti**clerical / **anti**climax / **anti**clockwise / **anti**coagulant / anti-competitive / **anti**-copying / **anti**-corruption / **anti**cyclone / **anti**depressant / **anti**-drug / **anti**-encroachment / **anti**-extremism / **anti**freeze / **anti**-globalization / **anti**-graft / **anti**gravity / **anti**-hate / **anti**-hero / **anti**-inflammatory / **anti**-liquor / **anti**-lock / **anti**-malarial / **anti**-national / **anti**oxidant / **anti**particle / **anti**-people / **anti**-personnel / **anti**perspirant / **anti**-poaching / **anti**pyretic / **anti**retroviral / **anti**-rowdy / **anti**-sabotage / **anti**septic / **anti**social / **anti**-stalking / **anti**tank / **anti**-terror / **anti**-terrorism / **anti**-theft / **anti**trust / **anti**viral / **anti**virus

******

ENGLISH SUFFIXES – A

-able

Used to form: adjectives, adverbs and nouns

General meaning: that can, should or must be done; having the characteristic of

Examples:

adaptable / agreeable / amenable / amicable / appreciable / approachable / assessable / avertable / avoidable / believable / breakable / calculable / changeable / chargeable / comfortable / companionable / computable / conceivable / controllable / curable / decipherable / declarable / desirable / detectable / detestable / doable / enjoyable / escapable / excitable / explainable / explicable / exploitable / fashionable / foreseeable / graspable / honorable / imaginable / imperturbable / indubitable / inevitable / justifiable / manageable / moveable / noticeable / observable / payable / pleasurable / portable / preventable / punishable / quantifiable / questionable / ratable / reachable / readable / reasonable / reckonable / recognizable / reliable / reputable / respectable / serviceable / sociable / stoppable / taxable / traceable / transferable / translatable / transportable / understandable / usable / utilizable / variable / washable / wearable / workable

******

-ability

Used to form: nouns
General meaning: a level of skill, intelligence, etc.
Example:
capability / curability / excitability / inescapability / inevitability / playability / preventability / serviceability / unavoidability / usability / workability

******

-ably

Used to form: adverbs

General meaning: skillful and well; in a particular manner

Examples:

aff**ably** / cap**ably** / charit**ably** / comfort**ably** / demonstr**ably** / indisput**ably** / inevit**ably** / irrit**ably** / not**ably** / notice**ably** / presum**ably** / prob**ably** / reason**ably** / remark**ably**

******

-acy

Used to form: nouns

General meaning: the position, quality, state or status of

Examples:

accur**acy** / adequ**acy** / delic**acy** / democr**acy** / intim**acy** / prim**acy** / priv**acy** / suprem**acy**

******

-ade

Used to form: nouns

General meaning: the state of; type of drink

Examples:

block**ade** / lemon**ade** / orange**ade**

******

-age

Used to form: nouns

General meaning: the action, condition, cost, result, state, etc. of

Examples:

anchor**age** / bond**age** / break**age** / cour**age** / mile**age** / post**age** / shrink**age** / suffr**age**

******

-aholic

Used to form: nouns
General meaning: liking something too much
Examples:
choc**aholic** / shop**aholic**

******

-al

Used to form: adjectives and nouns
General meaning: having the characteristic, condition or process of
Examples:
arriv**al** / carniv**al** / chronologic**al** / dispos**al** / magic**al** / rebutt**al** / referr**al** / remov**al** / surviv**al** / verb**al**

******

-alia

Used to form: nouns (plural)
General meaning: items relating to the particular activity
Examples:
kitchen**alia** / paraphern**alia**

******

-ally

Used to form: adverbs from adjectives that end in **-al**

General meaning: in a particular way

Examples:

dramatic**ally** / emotion**ally** / factu**ally** / histrionic**ally** / liter**ally** / magic**ally** / or**ally** / overemotion**ally** / radic**ally** / sensation**ally** / theatric**ally** / verb**ally** / voc**ally**

******

-an

Used to form: adjectives and nouns

General meaning: from; typical of; native of; an expert; fairly

Examples:

artis**an** / Afric**an** / Americ**an** / Morocc**an** / Mexic**an** / Chile**an** / Singapore**an** / Zimbabwe**an** / Keny**an** / Liby**an** / Paraguay**an** / Uruguay**an** / Angol**an** / Germ**an** / Ugand**an** / Sri Lank**an**

******

-ana

Used to form: nouns

General meaning: a collection of objects, facts, etc. related to the person, place, etc.

Examples:

Americ**ana** / Victor**iana**

******

-ance

Used to form: nouns

General meaning: the action or state of

Examples:

absorb**ance** / accept**ance** / admitt**ance** / annoy**ance** / appear**ance** / assist**ance** / attend**ance** / avoid**ance** / clear**ance** / conduct**ance** / deliver**ance** / disappear**ance** / dist**ance** / disturb**ance** / entr**ance** / expect**ance** / extravag**ance** / further**ance** / import**ance** / inst**ance** / insur**ance** / intend**ance** / intoler**ance** / observ**ance** / perform**ance** / resist**ance** / suffer**ance**

******

-ancy

Used to form: nouns

General meaning: the feature or state of

Examples:

account**ancy** / expect**ancy** / tru**ancy** / vac**ancy**

******

-ant

Used to form: adjectives and nouns

General meaning: that is or does something; having an effect

Examples:

contest**ant** / dorm**ant** / import**ant** / inhabit**ant** / lubric**ant** / pleas**ant** / reli**ant** / serv**ant** / signific**ant**

******

-ar

Used to form: adjectives and nouns

General meaning: the characteristic or state of

Examples:

burgl**ar** / circul**ar** / globul**ar** / rectangul**ar** / schol**ar** / singul**ar**

******

-arian

Used to form: adjectives and nouns

General meaning: believing in; involved in

Examples:

disciplin**arian** / humanit**arian**

******

-ard

Used to form: nouns

General meaning: a person or thing that has a particular characteristic

Examples:

drunk**ard** / wiz**ard**

******

-art

Used to form: nouns

General meaning: a person or thing that has a particular characteristic

Example:

bragg**art**

******

-ary

Used to form: adjectives and nouns

General meaning: having quality or characteristic of; related to

Examples:

budget**ary** / compliment**ary** / custom**ary** / deposit**ary** / diet**ary** / division**ary** / document**ary** / element**ary** / extraordin**ary** / function**ary** / institution**ary** / moment**ary** / parliament**ary** / planet**ary** / reaction**ary** / revision**ary** / revolution**ary** / second**ary** / secret**ary** / station**ary** / unit**ary**

******

-ate

Used to form: adjectives, nouns and verbs

General meaning: having the characteristic, function or status of

Examples:

activ**ate** / amelior**ate** / amput**ate** / consul**ate** / doctor**ate** / elabor**ate** / elector**ate** / hyphen**ate** / intric**ate** / Italian**ate** / motiv**ate** / passion**ate** / separ**ate** / stimul**ate** / viol**ate**

******

-ation

Used to form: nouns

General meaning: the action or state of

Examples:

alleg**ation** / alloc**ation** / alter**ation** / amplific**ation** / associ**ation** / calcul**ation** / celebr**ation** / circul**ation** / commemor**ation** / communic**ation** / connot**ation** / contamin**ation** / cre**ation** / declar**ation** / denunci**ation** / deterior**ation** / devast**ation** / disput**ation** / elimin**ation** / eradic**ation** / exagger**ation** / fascin**ation** / fortific**ation** / implic**ation** / indic**ation** / innov**ation** /

insinu**ation** / intensific**ation** / intim**ation** / magnific**ation** / manifest**ation** / migr**ation** / obliter**ation** / ornament**ation** / refut**ation** / rejuven**ation** / revel**ation** / rot**ation** / termin**ation** / transform**ation** / vac**ation** / vaccin**ation**

******

-ative

Used to form: adjectives

General meaning: showing tendency to do something

Examples:

argument**ative** / confirm**ative** / consult**ative** / expect**ative** / frequent**ative** / Illustr**ative** / inform**ative** / interpret**ative** / opinion**ative** / prevent**ative** / represent**ative** / talk**ative**

******

-atively

Used to form: adverbs

General meaning: in a particular way

Examples:

cre**atively** / imagin**atively** / innov**atively**

******

-ator

Used to form: nouns

General meaning: a person or thing that does something

Examples:

cre**ator** / initi**ator** / origin**ator** / percol**ator**

Prefixes and Suffixes -- B

ENGLISH PREFIXES – B

be-
Used to form: adjectives and verbs

General meaning: to cause or make

Examples:

becalmed / **be**dazzle / **be**devil / **be**fall / **be**fog / **be**friend / **be**loved / **be**moan / **be**mused / **be**reft / **be**set / **be**siege / **be**spatter / **be**speak / **be**spectacled / **be**stir / **be**stride / **be**take / **be**wail / **be**witch

******

by- (or bye-)
Used to form: nouns and verbs

General meaning: not much important; near

Examples:

by-product / **by**stander

******

ENGLISH SUFFIXES – B

-bian
Used to form: nouns

General meaning: living in a particular way

Example:

amphi**bian**

Prefixes and Suffixes -- C

ENGLISH PREFIXES – C

co-
Used to form: adjectives, adverbs, nouns and verbs
General meaning: accompanied by; together with
Examples:
co-activity / **co**-author / **co**-chairman / **co**-editor / **co**-education / **co**-existence / **co**-extension / **co**-factor / **co**-generation / **co**-housing / **co**incident / **co**operation / **co**-partner / **co**-payment / **co**-pilot / **co**-production / **co**-sized / **co**-star / **co**-worker

******

ENGLISH SUFFIXES – C

-centric
Used to form: adjectives
General meaning: deeply connected with a particular way of thinking; with a particular centre
Examples:
animal-**centric** / aviation-**centric** / border-**centric** / citizen-**centric** / commodity-**centric** / consumer-**centric** / customer-**centric** / data-**centric** / device-**centric** / ethno**centric** / euro**centric** / family-**centric** / geo**centric** / health-**centric** / immigration-**centric** / India-**centric** / IT-**centric** / kid-**centric** / mission-**centric** / mobile-**centric** / music-**centric** / passenger-

centric / patient-**centric** / performance-**centric** / policy-**centric** / privacy-**centric** / reform-**centric** / rural-**centric** / security-**centric** / startup-**centric** / technology-**centric** / urban-**centric** / user-**centric** / women-**centric**

******

-cy

Used to form: nouns

General meaning: the position, state, status or quality of

Examples:

accura**cy** / adequa**cy** / brillian**cy** / candida**cy** / chaplain**cy** / complica**cy** / delica**cy** / effica**cy** / efficien**cy** / elegan**cy** / equivalen**cy** / frequen**cy** / immedia**cy** / independen**cy** / infan**cy** / litera**cy** / permanen**cy** / pira**cy** / relevan**cy** / residen**cy** / secre**cy** / sufficien**cy**

Prefixes and Suffixes -- D

ENGLISH PREFIXES – D

de-

Used to form: adjectives, adverbs, nouns and verbs

General meaning: the opposite of; to take away something

Examples:

deactivate / **de**base / **de**caffeinated / **de**camp / **de**capitate / **de**celeration / **de**classify / **de**code / **de**commission / **de**compose / **de**compress / **de**congestant / **de**consecrate / **de**construct / **de**contaminate / **de**control / **de**couple / **de**fame / **de**forestation / **de**form / **de**frost / **de**generate / **de**grade / **de**hydrate / **de**-ice / **de**merge / **de**merit / **de**mist / **de**moralize / **de**plane / **de**populate / **de**rail / **de**regulate

******

demi-

Used to form: nouns

General meaning: half; partly

Examples:

demigod / **demi**monde

******

demo-

Used to form: adjectives, adverbs and nouns

General meaning: related to people

Examples:

democracy / **demo**cratic / **demo**graphy

******

dis-

Used to form: adjectives, adverbs, nouns and verbs

General meaning: not; the opposite of

Examples:

disability / **dis**able / **dis**abuse / **dis**advantage / **dis**affected / **dis**affiliate / **dis**agree / **dis**agreeable / **dis**agreeably / **dis**agreement / **dis**allow / **dis**ambiguate / **dis**appear / **dis**appoint / **dis**appointing / **dis**appointment / **dis**approval / **dis**approve / **dis**approving / **dis**arm / **dis**armament / **dis**arming / **dis**arrange / **dis**array / **dis**assemble / **dis**associate / **dis**band / **dis**bar / **dis**belief / **dis**believe / **dis**claim / **dis**closure / **dis**coloration / **dis**comfort / **dis**connected / **dis**consolate / **dis**content / **dis**contented / **dis**continue / **dis**continuous / **dis**courage / **dis**couragement / **dis**courteous / **dis**courtesy / **dis**creditable / **dis**entangle / **dis**equilibrium / **dis**grace / **dis**honest / **dis**honorable / **dis**incentive / **dis**inclined / **dis**infect / **dis**infectant / **dis**inherit / **dis**integrate / **dis**interest / **dis**invest / **dis**jointed / **dis**obedience / **dis**obedient / **dis**obey / **dis**obliging / **dis**order / **dis**orderly / **dis**organized / **dis**own / **dis**parity / **dis**passionate / **dis**place / **dis**please / **dis**pleasure / **dis**prove / **dis**qualify / **dis**quiet / **dis**regard / **dis**repair / **dis**reputable / **dis**repute / **dis**respect / **dis**robe / **dis**satisfaction / **dis**trust / **dis**unite / **dis**use

******

dys-

Used to form: adjectives, nouns and verbs

General meaning: abnormal

Examples:

dysfunction / **dys**functional / **dys**morphia / **dys**peptic / **dys**phoria / **dys**prosium / **dys**topia

******

ENGLISH SUFFIXES – D

-d

Used to form: adjectives

General meaning: having the characteristics of

Examples:

complicate**d** / marbl**ed** / sophisticate**d**

Used to form: past tense and past participle of regular verbs

Examples:

abuse**d** / accuse**d** / achieve**d** / acknowledge**d** / acquire**d** / admire**d** / advance**d** / advertise**d** / announce**d** / anticipate**d** / appreciate**d** / argue**d** / arrang**ed** / arrive**d** / associate**d** / assur**ed** / bake**d** / balance**d** / behave**d** / believe**d** / blame**d** / breathe**d** / calculate**d** / capture**d** / cause**d** / cease**d** / celebrate**d** / challeng**ed** / chang**ed** / charg**ed** / chase**d** / collapse**d** / combine**d** / communicate**d** / compare**d** / compete**d** / complete**d** / complicate**d** / concentrate**d** / conclude**d** / confine**d** / confuse**d** / continue**d** / contribute**d** / convince**d** / create**d** / curse**d** / damage**d** / dance**d** / dare**d** / debate**d** / decide**d** / declare**d** / decline**d** / decorate**d** / decrease**d** / define**d** / demonstrate**d** /

derived / described / determined / devoted / disapproved / dissolved / distributed / divided / dominated / eased / educated / emerged / enabled / encouraged / engaged / ensured / escaped / estimated / exaggerated / examined / exchanged / excluded / excused / exercised / experienced / exploded / explored / exposed / featured / figured / financed / forced / framed / gambled / generated / glued / guided / handled / hided / hired / hoped / ignored / illustrated / imagined / imposed / improved / included / increased / indicated / influenced / injured / introduced / investigated / invited / involved / issued / joked / judged / located / managed / manufactured / measured / moved / named / noticed / observed / operated / opposed / outlined / paused / persuaded / piled / placed / posed / praised / prepared / preserved / produced / promoted / pronounced / proposed / proved / provided / purchased / pursued / raced / raised / received / reduced / refused / related / released / removed / replaced / reproduced / required / rescued / reserved / resolved / restored / retired / reversed / revised / ruled / saved / scared / scored / secured / separated / served / settled / shared / shined / singed / sliced / smiled / smoked / solved / squeezed / stared / stored / struggled / substituted / survived / tackled / tasted / traced / traded / translated / tuned / typed / united / urged / used / valued / ventured / voted / waked / wasted / waved / weaved / welcomed / whistled / writhed

******

-dom

Used to form: nouns

General meaning: the state, group or rule of

Examples:

free**dom** / king**dom** / martyr**dom** / official**dom**

Prefixes and Suffixes -- E

ENGLISH PREFIXES – E

em-
Used to form: verbs
General meaning: to put into a particular condition, etc.; to cause to be
Examples:
embalm / **em**bolden / **em**power

******

en-
Used to form: verbs
General meaning: to put into a particular condition, etc.; to cause to be
Examples:
encase / **en**code / **en**danger / **en**large

******

ex-
Used to form: nouns
General meaning: previous
Examples:
ex-minister / **ex-**president / **ex-**student / **ex-**wife

******

extra-

Used to form: adjectives

General meaning: beyond; unusual

Examples:

extrajudicial / **extra**marital / **extra**ordinary / **extra**-sensory /
extra-solar / **extra**-special / **extra**terrestrial / **extra**-thin

******

ENGLISH SUFFIXES – E

-ed

Used to form: adjectives

General meaning: having the characteristics of

Example:

wood**ed**

Used to form: past tense and past participle of regular verbs

Examples:

absorb**ed** / accept**ed** / account**ed** / act**ed** / adapt**ed** / add**ed** /
address**ed** / adjust**ed** / adopt**ed** / annoy**ed** / answer**ed** /
appeal**ed** / appear**ed** / appoint**ed** / approach**ed** / arrest**ed** /
ask**ed** / assist**ed** / attach**ed** / attack**ed** / attempt**ed** / attend**ed** /
attract**ed** / avoid**ed** / award**ed** / bash**ed** / belong**ed** / bend**ed** /
block**ed** / board**ed** / boil**ed** / bomb**ed** / book**ed** / borrow**ed** /
bother**ed** / broadcast**ed** / brush**ed** / burn**ed** / call**ed** / camp**ed** /
cheat**ed** / check**ed** / chew**ed** / claim**ed** / clean**ed** / clear**ed** /
click**ed** / climb**ed** / collect**ed** / command**ed** / comment**ed** /
complain**ed** / conduct**ed** / confirm**ed** / conflict**ed** / confront**ed** /
connect**ed** / consider**ed** / construct**ed** / consult**ed** / contact**ed** /

contained / contracted / contrasted / converted / cooked / cooled / corrected / coughed / counted / covered / cracked / crashed / crossed / crushed / curbed / decayed / defeated / defended / delayed / delivered / demanded / depended / deposited / depressed / deserted / designed / destroyed / directed / disappeared / disappointed / discussed / dismissed / displayed / distinguished / disturbed / doubted / dressed / dumped / dusted / developed / earned / elected / embarrassed / employed / encountered / ended / enjoyed / entered / established / exhibited / expanded / expected / experimented / explained / exported / expressed / extended / failed / fastened / feared / fetched / filled / filmed / finished / fixed / flashed / floated / flooded / flowed / focused / folded / forecasted / formed / functioned / funded / gained / gathered / governed / granted / guarded / guessed / handed / hanged / happened / harmed / healed / heated / helped / highlighted / hosted / hunted / imported / infected / informed / inserted / insisted / installed / insulted / intended / interpreted / interrupted / interviewed / invented / invested / ironed / joined / jumped / kicked / killed / knocked / lacked / landed / laughed / launched / leaned / learned / lifted / limited / linked / listed / listened / livened / loaded / locked / looked / mailed / maintained / marched / marked / matched / melted / mentioned / minded / missed / mixed / monitored / mounted / obeyed / objected / obtained / offended / offered / opened / ordered / packed / painted / parked / passed / performed / photographed / picked / planted / played / pointed / polished / posted / poured / predicted / pressed / pretended / prevented / printed / proceeded / processed / progressed / projected / protected /

protest**ed** / publish**ed** / pull**ed** / punch**ed** / punish**ed** / push**ed** / question**ed** / rain**ed** / reach**ed** / react**ed** / recall**ed** / recommend**ed** / record**ed** / recover**ed** / reflect**ed** / reform**ed** / register**ed** / reject**ed** / relax**ed** / remain**ed** / remark**ed** / remember**ed** / remind**ed** / rent**ed** / repair**ed** / repeat**ed** / report**ed** / represent**ed** / request**ed** / resist**ed** / respect**ed** / respond**ed** / rest**ed** / restrict**ed** / result**ed** / retain**ed** / return**ed** / reveal**ed** / review**ed** / reward**ed** / ring**ed** / risk**ed** / roll**ed** / ruin**ed** / rush**ed** / sail**ed** / scratch**ed** / scream**ed** / seal**ed** / search**ed** / select**ed** / shift**ed** / shout**ed** / show**ed** / sign**ed** / smash**ed** / smell**ed** / snow**ed** / sort**ed** / sound**ed** / spell**ed** / spoil**ed** / spray**ed** / stamp**ed** / start**ed** / stay**ed** / steer**ed** / stress**ed** / stretch**ed** / succeed**ed** / suck**ed** / suffer**ed** / suggest**ed** / support**ed** / surround**ed** / survey**ed** / suspect**ed** / swallow**ed** / sweat**ed** / swell**ed** / switch**ed** / talk**ed** / test**ed** / thank**ed** / threaten**ed** / touch**ed** / tour**ed** / train**ed** / transform**ed** / transport**ed** / treat**ed** / trick**ed** / trust**ed** / turn**ed** / twist**ed** / view**ed** / visit**ed** / wait**ed** / walk**ed** / wander**ed** / want**ed** / warm**ed** / warn**ed** / wash**ed** / watch**ed** / waver**ed** / weigh**ed** / whisper**ed** / wish**ed** / witness**ed** / wonder**ed** / work**ed** / yawn**ed**

******

-ee

Used to form: nouns
General meaning: a person affected by or concerned with
Examples:
absent**ee** / address**ee** / employ**ee** / interview**ee** / refug**ee** / train**ee**

******

-eer

Used to form: nouns and verbs

General meaning: a person concerned with

Examples:

auction**eer** / command**eer**

******

-en

Used to form: adjectives and verbs

General meaning: to become; to make; made of; similar to

Examples:

black**en** / bright**en** / broad**en** / damp**en** / dark**en** / flatt**en** / fresh**en** / fright**en** / gladd**en** / gold**en** / hard**en** / heart**en** / length**en** / less**en** / light**en** / loos**en** / moist**en** / quick**en** / rip**en** / sadd**en** / sharp**en** / short**en** / slack**en** / soft**en** / strength**en** / sweet**en** / thick**en** / threat**en** / tight**en** / tough**en** / weak**en** / wid**en** / wood**en**

******

-ence

Used to form: nouns

General meaning: the action or state of

Examples:

abstin**ence** / confid**ence** / depend**ence** / differ**ence** / diverg**ence** / emerg**ence** / fraudul**ence** / indulg**ence** / prud**ence**

******

-ency

Used to form: nouns

General meaning: the characteristic or state of

Examples:

complac**ency** / depend**ency** / lat**ency**

******

-ent

Used to form: adjectives and nouns

General meaning: that is or does something

Examples:

depend**ent** / deterr**ent** / differ**ent** / adher**ent** / oppon**ent**

******

-er

Used to form: nouns

General meaning: a person or thing with a particular characteristic; connected with profession

Examples:

admir**er** / advertis**er** / assault**er** / astronom**er** / attack**er** / back**er** / broadcast**er** / buy**er** / command**er** / comput**er** / conjur**er** / consum**er** / contain**er** / danc**er** / deal**er** / design**er** / discover**er** / driv**er** / dry**er** / employ**er** / examin**er** / follow**er** / foreign**er** / gambl**er** / hold**er** / intrud**er** / lead**er** / lectur**er** / manag**er** / mugg**er** / offic**er** / organiz**er** / own**er** / paint**er** / perform**er** / philosoph**er** / pray**er** / present**er** / procur**er** / promot**er** / prowl**er** / raid**er** / research**er** / retail**er** / review**er** / rul**er** / scrap**er** / settl**er** /

singer / stalker / stranger / supporter / trader / trainer / traveler / vacationer / voyager / worker

Used to form: comparative adjectives and adverbs
Examples:
abler / better / bigger / blacker / blunter / bolder / braver / brighter / busier / cheaper / cleaner / clearer / cleverer / colder / commoner / cooler / costlier / darker / dearer / deeper / dimmer / dirtier / drier / easier / fairer / farther / faster / fatter / finer / funnier / greater / greener / happier / harder / healthier / heavier / higher / hotter / kinder / larger / lazier / lighter / likelier / longer / lower / luckier / madder / merrier / narrower / naughtier / nearer / newer / nicer / nobler / noisier / paler / poorer / prettier / prouder / quicker / quieter / redder / richer / sadder / safer / shallower / sharper / shorter / simpler / slower / smaller / smoother / sooner / stronger / sweeter / taller / thicker / thinner / tinier / tougher / uglier / warmer / wealthier / wetter / whiter / wider / wilder / wiser / younger

******

-ery

Used to form: nouns
General meaning: the characteristic, group, state or practice of; a place where something is prepared, etc.
Examples:
archery / bakery / bravery / cookery / fishery / greenery / orangery / perfumery / shrubbery

******

-ese

Used to form: adjectives and nouns

General meaning: of a country, etc; the style or language of

Examples:

Bhutan**ese** / Chinese / Congol**ese** / Japan**ese** / journal**ese** / Myanmar**ese** / Nepal**ese** / official**ese** / Senegal**ese** / Sudan**ese** / Togol**ese** / Vienn**ese** / Vietnam**ese**

******

-esque

Used to form: adjectives

General meaning: in the fashion of

Examples:

Kafka**esque** / statu**esque**

******

-ess

Used to form: nouns

General meaning: female

Examples:

act**ess** / author**ess** / enchantr**ess** / lion**ess** / seamstr**ess** / steward**ess** / waitr**ess**

******

-est

Used to form: superlative adjectives and adverbs

Examples:

ablest / biggest / blackest / bluntest / boldest / bravest / brightest / busiest / cheapest / cleanest / clearest / cleverest / coldest / coolest / costliest / darkest / dearest / deepest / dimmest / dirtiest / driest / easiest / eldest / fairest / farthest / fastest / fattest / finest / funniest / greatest / greenest / happiest / hardest / healthiest / heaviest / highest / hottest / kindest / largest / latest / laziest / lightest / longest / lowest / luckiest / maddest / merriest / narrowest / naughtiest / nearest / newest / nicest / noblest / noisiest / oldest / palest / poorest / prettiest / proudest / quickest / reddest / richest / saddest / safest / shallowest / sharpest / sharpest / shortest / shyest / simplest / slowest / smallest / smoothest / soonest / strongest / sweetest / tallest / thickest / thinnest / tiniest / toughest / ugliest / warmest / wealthiest / wettest / whitest / widest / wildest / wisest / youngest

******

-ey

Used to form: adjectives and nouns

General meaning: full of; having the characteristic of

Examples:

clayey / gooey

Prefixes and Suffixes -- F

ENGLISH SUFFIXES – F

-fold

Used to form: adjectives and adverbs

General meaning: multiplied by

Examples:

five**fold** / hundred**fold** / ten**fold**

******

-ful

Used to form: adjectives and nouns

General meaning: full of; having the characteristics of

Examples:

bag**ful** / bash**ful** / blush**ful** / bottle**ful** / bowl**ful** / care**ful** / cheer**ful** / color**ful** / delight**ful** / despite**ful** / disgrace**ful** / disgust**ful** / dish**ful** / distrust**ful** / doubt**ful** / faith**ful** / fear**ful** / force**ful** / forget**ful** / fork**ful** / fret**ful** / gain**ful** / grate**ful** / harm**ful** / hate**ful** / health**ful** / help**ful** / hope**ful** / house**ful** / hurt**ful** / impact**ful** / joy**ful** / neglect**ful** / pain**ful** / peace**ful** / plate**ful** / play**ful** / pocket**ful** / power**ful** / praise**ful** / purpose**ful** / regard**ful** / resource**ful** / respect**ful** / rest**ful** / shame**ful** / skill**ful** / sorrow**ful** / spite**ful** / stress**ful** / success**ful** / table**ful** / tear**ful** / thank**ful** / thought**ful** / trust**ful** / truth**ful** / use**ful** / waste**ful** / watch**ful** / will**ful** / wish**ful** wonder**ful** / youth**ful**

Prefixes and Suffixes -- G

ENGLISH PREFIXES – G

glyc-

Used to form: noun

General meaning: relating to compounds with glycerin

Examples:

glyceride

******

ENGLISH SUFFIXES – G

-gen

Used to form: noun

General meaning: that generates or produces

Examples:

hydro**gen** / oxy**gen** / patho**gen**

Prefixes and Suffixes -- H

ENGLISH PREFIXES – H

hydro-
Used to form: nouns
General meaning: containing hydrogen; relating to water
Examples:
hydrocarbon / **hydro**electric / **hydro**genated / **hydro**logy /
hydrolysis / **hydro**phobia / **hydro**plane / **hydro**ponics /
hydrosphere / **hydro**therapy

******

hyper-
Used to form: adjective, nouns and verbs
General meaning: having too much
Examples:
hyperactive / **hyper**baric / **hyper**bola / **hyper**correction /
hypercritical / **hyper**inflation / **hyper**link / **hyper**market /
hypermedia / **hyper**sensitive / **hyper**text / **hyper**trophy /
hyperventilate

******

hypo-
Used to form: adjective, nouns
General meaning: under something; below average
Examples:
hypodermic / **hypo**thermia / **hypo**thyroidism / **hypo**xia

******

ENGLISH SUFFIXES – H

-head

Used to form: nouns

General meaning: addicted or enthusiastic person

gear**head** / smack**head**

******

-hood

Used to form: nouns

General meaning: the condition, period or state of

adult**hood** / baby**hood** / boy**hood** / brother**hood** / child**hood** / false**hood** / father**hood** / likeli**hood** / mother**hood** / neighbor**hood** / parent**hood** / priest**hood** / woman**hood**

Prefixes and Suffixes -- I

ENGLISH PREFIXES – I

im-

Used to form: adjectives, adverbs and nouns

General meaning: not; the opposite of

Examples:

immaterial / **im**mature / **im**measurable / **im**memorial / **im**migrant / **im**mobile / **im**moderate / **im**modest / **im**moral / **im**morally / **im**mortal / **im**movable / **im**passable / **im**patient / **im**perceptible / **im**perfect / **im**perishable / **im**permanent / **im**permeable / **im**permissible / **im**personal / **im**pious / **im**plausible / **im**polite / **im**practical / **im**probable / **im**prudent / **im**pure

******

in-

Used to form: adjectives, adverbs and nouns

General meaning: not; the opposite of

Examples:

inaccurate / **in**action / **in**activate / **in**adequate / **in**admissible / **in**advertent / **in**advisable / **in**alienable / **in**animate / **in**applicable / **in**appropriate / **in**articulate / **in**attention / **in**audible / **in**auspicious / **in**authentic / **in**calculable / **in**capable / **in**capacity / **in**cautious / **in**coherent / **in**commensurate / **in**comparable / **in**compatible / **in**competent / **in**complete / **in**comprehensible / **in**comprehension / **in**conceivable / **in**conclusive / **in**consistent / **in**conspicuous / **in**constant / **in**contestable / **in**convenience / **in**corporeal /

incorruptible / indecency / indecisive / indefinable / indefinite / independent / indescribable / indestructible / indeterminate / indigestible / indignity / indirect / indiscipline / indiscreet / indispensable / indisputable / indissoluble / indistinguishable / inedible / ineffective / inefficient / inelegant / ineptitude / inequality / inequitable / ineradicable / inescapable / inessential / inestimable / inexact / inexcusable / inexpedient / inexpensive / inexperience / inexpert / infallible / infamous / infinite / ingratitude / inhuman / injustice / innumerate / inoffensive / inoperable / insecure / insincere / instability / insubstantial / insufficient / intemperate / intransitive / invalidate

******

inter-

Used to form: adjectives, adverbs, nouns and verbs
General meaning: between; linking; from one to another, not within
Examples:
interact / interaction / interactive / interbreed / interchange / interconnect / intercontinental / intercultural / intercut / interdenominational / interdepartmental / interdependent / interdisciplinary / interface / interfaith / interfere / intergalactic / intergenerational / intergovernmental / interject / interlace / interleave / interlink / interlock / interloper / interlude / intermarry / intermediary / intermingle / intermix / internecine / interpenetrate / interpersonal / interplanetary / interracial / interrelate / intersect / intersperse / interstate / interstellar / intertwine

******

intra-

Used to form: adjectives and adverbs

General meaning: within

Examples:

intra-departmental / intramural / intramuscular / intranet / intrauterine / intravenous

******

ir-

Used to form: adjectives, adverbs and nouns

General meaning: not; the opposite of

Examples:

irrational / irrecoverable / irreducible / irrefutable / irregular / irregularity / irrelevance / irreligious / irremediable / irreplaceable / irresponsible / irretrievable / irreverent

******

ENGLISH SUFFIXES – I

-ial

Used to form: adjectives

General meaning: typical of

Examples:

denial / dictatorial / territorial

******

-ially

Used to form: adverbs

General meaning: in a particular way

Examples:

artificially / commercially / crucially / especially / essentially / financially / industrially / initially / materially / officially / partially / potentially / socially / substantially

******

-ian

Used to form: adjectives and nouns

General meaning: from; typical of; native of; an expert; fairly

Examples:

Albanian / Algerian / Armenian / Athenian / Australian / Austrian / Bostonian / Brazilian / Brazilian / Bulgarian / Californian / Canadian / Colombian / Egyptian / guardian / historian / Hungarian / Indian / Italian / Jordanian / Liberian / magician / Malaysian / Maldivian / mathematician / Mauritian / Mongolian / Romanian / Russian / Saudi Arabian / Serbian / Shakespearian / Slovakian / Slovenian / Syrian / Trinidadian / Ukrainian / Zambian

******

-ibility

Used to form: nouns

General meaning: a level of skill or intelligence

Examples:

feasibility / plausibility / responsibility

******

-ible

Used to form: adjectives

General meaning: that can, should or must be; having the characteristic of

Examples:

accessible / audible / collapsible / collectible / comprehensible / convertible / credible / defensible / digestible / discernible / expressible / feasible / forcible / gullible / horrible / implausible / intelligible / perceptible / plausible / reprehensible / responsible / reversible / susceptible / terrible

******

-ibly

Used to form: adverbs

General meaning: in a particular way

Examples:

forcibly / horribly / impossibly / incredibly / responsibly / sensibly / terribly / visibly

******

-ic

Used to form: adjectives and nouns

General meaning: having the characteristic of; related to

Examples:

Arabic / economic / electric / horrific / linguistic / photographic / poetic / scenic / specific

******

-ical

Used to form: adjectives

General meaning: having the characteristic of

Examples:

categorical / comical / electrical / historical / logical / medical / musical / physical / political / technical / tropical

******

-ically

Used to form: adverbs

General meaning: connected with

Examples:

dramatically / physically / radically

******

-ics

Used to form: nouns

General meaning: the study of

Examples:

athletics / dramatics / electronics / genetics / physics

******

-ide

Used to form: nouns

General meaning: a compound of

Examples:

boride /chloride / fluoride

******

-ient

Used to form: adjectives

General meaning: having the characteristic of

Examples:

conven**ient** / defic**ient** / effic**ient** / exped**ient** / profic**ient** / suffic**ient**

******

-ify

Used to form: verbs

General meaning: to make or become

Examples:

clar**ify** / detox**ify** / pur**ify** / simpl**ify** / solid**ify**

******

-ing

General meaning: used to make the present participle of regular verbs

Examples:

absorb**ing** / abus**ing** / accept**ing** / accompany**ing** / account**ing** / accus**ing** / achiev**ing** / acknowledg**ing** / acquir**ing** / act**ing** / adapt**ing** / add**ing** / address**ing** / adjust**ing** / admir**ing** / admitt**ing** / adopt**ing** / advanc**ing** / advertis**ing** / announc**ing** / annoy**ing** / answer**ing** / anticipat**ing** / appeal**ing** / appear**ing** / apply**ing** / appoint**ing** / appreciat**ing** / approach**ing** / argu**ing** / aris**ing** / arrang**ing** / arrest**ing** / arriv**ing** / ask**ing** / assist**ing** / associat**ing** /

assuring / attaching / attacking / attempting / attending /
attracting / avoiding / awarding / baking / balancing / banning /
bashing / bearing / beating / becoming / beginning / behaving /
believing / belonging / bending / benefiting / betting / biding /
biting / blaming / blocking / blowing / boarding / boiling /
bombing / booking / borrowing / bothering / breaking /
breathing / bringing / broadcasting / brushing / building /
burning / bursting / burying / buying / calculating / calling /
camping / canceling / capturing / carrying / casting / catching /
causing / ceasing / celebrating / challenging / changing /
charging / chasing / chatting / cheating / checking / chewing /
choosing / chopping / claiming / clapping / cleaning / clearing /
clicking / climbing / collapsing / collecting / combining / coming
/ commanding / commenting / committing / communicating /
comparing / competing / complaining / completing / complicating
/ concentrating / concluding / conducting / confining / confirming
/ conflicting / confronting / confusing / connecting / considering /
constructing / consulting / contacting / containing / continuing /
contracting / contrasting / contributing / controlling / converting
/ convincing / cooking / cooling / copying / correcting / costing /
coughing / counting / covering / cracking / crashing / creating /
crossing / crushing / crying / curbing / cursing / cutting /
damaging / dancing / daring / dealing / debating / decaying /
deciding / declaring / declining / decorating / decreasing /
defeating / defending / defining / delaying / delivering /
demanding / demonstrating / denying / depending / depositing /
depressing / deriving / describing / deserting / designing /
destroying / determining / developing / devoting / digging /
directing / disagreeing / disappearing / disappointing /

disapprov**ing** / discuss**ing** / dismiss**ing** / display**ing** / dissolv**ing** / distinguish**ing** / distribut**ing** / disturb**ing** / divid**ing** / dominat**ing** / doubt**ing** / dragg**ing** / draw**ing** / dream**ing** / dress**ing** / drink**ing** / dropp**ing** / dry**ing** / dump**ing** / dust**ing** / dye**ing** / earn**ing** / eas**ing** / eat**ing** / educat**ing** / elect**ing** / embarrass**ing** / emerg**ing** / employ**ing** / empty**ing** / enabl**ing** / encounter**ing** / encourag**ing** / end**ing** / engag**ing** / enjoy**ing** / ensur**ing** / enter**ing** / escap**ing** / establish**ing** / estimat**ing** / exaggerat**ing** / examin**ing** / exchang**ing** / exclud**ing** / excus**ing** / exercis**ing** / exhibit**ing** / expand**ing** / expect**ing** / experienc**ing** / experiment**ing** / explain**ing** / explod**ing** / explor**ing** / export**ing** / expos**ing** / express**ing** / extend**ing** / fac**ing** / fail**ing** / fancy**ing** / fasten**ing** / fear**ing** / featur**ing** / feed**ing** / feel**ing** / fetch**ing** / fight**ing** / figur**ing** / fill**ing** / film**ing** / financ**ing** / find**ing** / finish**ing** / fir**ing** / fix**ing** / flash**ing** / float**ing** / flood**ing** / flow**ing** / fly**ing** / focus**ing** / fold**ing** / forc**ing** / forecast**ing** / forgett**ing** / forgiv**ing** / form**ing** / fram**ing** / freez**ing** / fry**ing** / function**ing** / fund**ing** / gain**ing** / gambl**ing** / garden**ing** / gather**ing** / generat**ing** / gett**ing** / giv**ing** / glu**ing** / go**ing** / govern**ing** / grabb**ing** / grant**ing** / grow**ing** / guard**ing** / guess**ing** / guid**ing** / hand**ing** / handl**ing** / hang**ing** / happen**ing** / harm**ing** / heal**ing** / hear**ing** / heat**ing** / help**ing** / hid**ing** / highlight**ing** / hir**ing** / hitt**ing** / hold**ing** / hop**ing** / host**ing** / hunt**ing** / hurry**ing** / hurt**ing** / identify**ing** / ignor**ing** / illustrat**ing** / imagin**ing** / imply**ing** / import**ing** / impos**ing** / improv**ing** / includ**ing** / increas**ing** / indicat**ing** / infect**ing** / influenc**ing** / inform**ing** / injur**ing** / insert**ing** / insist**ing** / install**ing** / insult**ing** / intend**ing** / interpret**ing** / interrupt**ing** / interview**ing** / introduc**ing** / invent**ing** / investigat**ing** / invest**ing** / invit**ing** / involv**ing** / iron**ing** / issu**ing** / join**ing** / jok**ing** / judg**ing** / jump**ing**

/ justifying / keeping / kicking / killing / knitting / knocking / knowing / labeling / lacking / landing / laughing / launching / laying / leading / leaning / learning / leaving / lending / letting / lifting / limiting / linking / listening / listing / livening / loading / locating / locking / looking / loosing / lying / mailing / maintaining / making / managing / manufacturing / marching / marking / marrying / matching / measuring / meeting / melting / mentioning / minding / missing / mistaking / mixing / monitoring / mounting / moving / multiplying / naming / noticing / obeying / objecting / observing / obtaining / occupying / occurring / offending / offering / opening / operating / opposing / ordering / outlining / overcoming / packing / painting / parking / passing / pausing / paying / performing / permitting / persuading / photocopying / photographing / picking / piling / placing / planning / planting / playing / plotting / pointing / polishing / posing / posting / pouring / practicing / praising / predicting / preferring / preparing / preserving / pressing / pretending / preventing / printing / proceeding / processing / producing / progressing / projecting / promoting / pronouncing / proposing / protecting / protesting / providing / proving / publishing / pulling / punching / punishing / purchasing / pursuing / pushing / putting / qualifying / questioning / quitting / racing / raining / raising / reaching / reacting / reading / recalling / receiving / recommending / recording / recovering / reducing / referring / reflecting / reforming / refusing / registering / regretting / rejecting / relating / relaxing / releasing / relying / remaining / remarking / remembering / reminding / removing / renting / repairing / repeating / replacing / replying / reporting / representing / reproducing / requesting / requiring /

rescu**ing** / reserv**ing** / resist**ing** / resolv**ing** / respect**ing** / respond**ing** / rest**ing** / restor**ing** / restrict**ing** / result**ing** / retain**ing** / retir**ing** / return**ing** / reveal**ing** / revers**ing** / review**ing** / revis**ing** / reward**ing** / rid**ing** / ring**ing** / ris**ing** / risk**ing** / robb**ing** / roll**ing** / rubb**ing** / ruin**ing** / rul**ing** / runn**ing** / rush**ing** / sail**ing** / satisfy**ing** / sav**ing** / say**ing** / scar**ing** / scor**ing** / scratch**ing** / scream**ing** / seal**ing** / search**ing** / secur**ing** / see**ing** / seek**ing** / select**ing** / sell**ing** / send**ing** / separat**ing** / serv**ing** / settl**ing** / shak**ing** / shar**ing** / shift**ing** / shin**ing** / shoot**ing** / shout**ing** / show**ing** / shutt**ing** / signal**ing** / sign**ing** / sing**ing** / sink**ing** / sitt**ing** / sleep**ing** / slic**ing** / slipp**ing** / smash**ing** / smell**ing** / smil**ing** / smok**ing** / snow**ing** / solv**ing** / sort**ing** / sound**ing** / speak**ing** / spell**ing** / spend**ing** / spinn**ing** / splitt**ing** / spoil**ing** / spray**ing** / spread**ing** / squeez**ing** / stamp**ing** / stand**ing** / star**ing** / start**ing** / stay**ing** / steal**ing** / steer**ing** / stepp**ing** / stick**ing** / sting**ing** / stopp**ing** / stor**ing** / stress**ing** / stretch**ing** / strik**ing** / strip**ing** / struggl**ing** / study**ing** / substitut**ing** / succeed**ing** / suck**ing** / suffer**ing** / suggest**ing** / supply**ing** / support**ing** / surround**ing** / survey**ing** / surviv**ing** / suspect**ing** / swallow**ing** / swear**ing** / sweat**ing** / sweep**ing** / swell**ing** / swimm**ing** / swing**ing** / switch**ing** / tackl**ing** / tak**ing** / talk**ing** / tast**ing** / teach**ing** / tell**ing** / tend**ing** / test**ing** / thank**ing** / think**ing** / threaten**ing** / throw**ing** / toe**ing** / touch**ing** / tour**ing** / trac**ing** / trad**ing** / train**ing** / transferr**ing** / transform**ing** / translat**ing** / transport**ing** / trapp**ing** / travel**ing** / treat**ing** / trick**ing** / tripp**ing** / trust**ing** / try**ing** / tun**ing** / turn**ing** / twist**ing** / typ**ing** / understand**ing** / undo**ing** / unit**ing** / unload**ing** / upsett**ing** / urg**ing** / us**ing** / valu**ing** / vary**ing** / ventur**ing** / view**ing** / visit**ing** / vot**ing** / wait**ing** / wak**ing** / walk**ing** /

wandering / wanting / warming / warning / washing / wasting /
watching / wavering / waving / wearing / weaving / weighing /
welcoming / whispering / whistling / winding / wining /
withdrawing / witnessing / wondering / working / worrying /
worshiping / wounding / wrapping / writhing / writing / yawning

******

-ion

Used to form: nouns

General meaning: the action or state of

Examples:

absorption / accession / accommodation / action / adaption /
addition / admiration / adoption / application / assertion /
association / attention / attraction / calculation / capitulation /
celebration / collection / combination / communication /
competition / concentration / conception / conclusion /
conduction / confliction / connection / consideration /
construction / contention / contraction / contradiction /
contribution / convention / conversation / correction / criterion
/ decoration / deposition / depression / description / destruction
/ determination / direction / discussion / dissection /
distribution / division / education / election / exaction /
examination / exception / exclamation / exhibition / expectation
/ explanation / explosion / expression / extension / fruition /
generation / hesitation / imagination / impaction / implication /
impression / indication / infection / information / insertion /
instruction / interruption / introduction / invention /
investigation / invitation / location / objection / observation /

operation / opinion / opposition / option / perfection / permission / pollution / population / possession / prediction / preparation / presentation / prevention / production / profession / progression / projection / promotion / pronunciation / proposition / protection / publication / punctuation / qualification / quotation / recognition / reduction / reflection / regulation / rejection / reputation / reservation / resolution / restriction / revision / revolution / satisfaction / secretion / selection / situation / subjection / succession / suggestion / suspicion / vacation / variation

******

-ish

Used to form: adjectives
General meaning: having the characteristic of; native of; approximately
Examples:
bookish / childish / Danish / Finnish / Polish / reddish / Swedish / Swish / thirtyish / Turkish

******

-ishly

Used to form: adverbs
Examples: in a particular way
babyishly / childishly / foolishly

******

-ism

Used to form: noun

General meaning: the action, characteristic, movement, result, state or system of; unfair treatment; a medical condition

Examples:

activism / aestheticism / agrarianism / altruism / Americanism / anarchism / antiquarianism / atheism / athleticism / authoritarianism / autism / baptism / Buddhism / cannibalism / capitalism / centralism / classicism / clericalism / collectivism / colloquialism / commercialism / communism / conformism / creationism / criticism / cronyism / dogmatism / elitism / embolism / euphemism / evangelism / exhibitionism / exorcism / expansionism / extremism / fanaticism / fatalism / favoritism / federalism / feminism / feudalism / fundamentalism / futurism / heroism / Hinduism / hooliganism / humanism / hypnotism / idealism / imperialism / impressionism / legalism / liberalism / lyricism / magnetism / materialism / mercantilism / metabolism / metamorphism / microorganism / militarism / modernism / monotheism / multiculturalism / multilingualism / mutualism / nationalism / neoclassicism / neologism / nepotism / pacifism / parochialism / paternalism / patriotism / perfectionism / pessimism / plagiarism / pluralism / pragmatism / provincialism / pugilism / racism / realism / regionalism / relativism / rheumatism / ritualism / sadism / secularism / separatism / sexism / skepticism / surrealism / terrorism / theism / truism / unionism / utilitarianism / vandalism / vegetarianism

******

-ist
Used to form: adjectives and nouns

General meaning: a person with a particular belief; a person who is engaged in a particular activity

Examples:

anarch**ist** / athe**ist** / conceptual**ist** / conform**ist** / dent**ist** / nihil**ist** / plagiar**ist** / violin**ist**

******

-ition

Used to form: nouns

General meaning: the action or state of

Examples:

add**ition** / compet**ition** / contr**ition** / demol**ition** / exhib**ition** / oppos**ition**

******

-ity

Used to form: nouns

General meaning: the characteristic or state of

Examples:

creativ**ity** / dependabil**ity** / disun**ity** / equal**ity** /fidel**ity** / impur**ity** / odd**ity** / pur**ity** / reliabil**ity** / san**ity** / similar**ity** / uniform**ity**

******

-ive

Used to form: adjectives and nouns

General meaning: tending to; having the nature of

Examples:

descript**ive** / explet**ive** / explos**ive** / invas**ive** / mot**ive**

******

-ization (-isation)

Used to form: nouns

General meaning: the state of

Example:

categor**ization** / colon**ization** / decentral**ization** / dehuman**ization** / democrat**ization** / demoral**ization** / desensit**ization** / mobil**ization** / modern**ization**

******

-izationally (-isationally)

Used to form: adverbs

General meaning: in a particular way

Example:

organ**izationally**

******

-ize (-ise)

Used to form: verbs

General meaning: to become or make; to talk, think, treat, work, etc. in a particular way; to put in

Examples:

American**ize** / anglic**ize** / central**ize** / critic**ize** / decentral**ize** / deput**ize** / fossil**ize** / hospital**ize** / pasteur**ize** / privat**ize** / public**ize** / regional**ize** / theor**ize**

Prefixes and Suffixes -- J

ENGLISH PREFIXES – J

juxta-

Used to form: noun, verb

General meaning: near

Example:

juxtapose / **juxta**-vesicular

******

ENGLISH SUFFIXES – J

-ject

Used to form: verb

General meaning: to throw

Example:

e**ject** / in**ject** / inter**ject**

Prefixes and Suffixes -- K

ENGLISH PREFIXES – K

konio-

Used to form: noun

General meaning: relating to dust

Example:

koniology

******

ENGLISH SUFFIXES – K

-kinesis

Used to form: noun

General meaning: relating to motion

Example:

cyto**kinesis**

Prefixes and Suffixes -- L

ENGLISH PREFIXES – L

lymph-
Used to form: noun
General meaning: relating to lymph
Examples:
lymphocyte / **lympho**ma

******

ENGLISH SUFFIXES – L

-less
Used to form: adjectives
General meaning: without; unaffected by
Examples:
age**less** / breath**less** / care**less** / change**less** / child**less** /
cloud**less** / defense**less** / effort**less** / fear**less** / flavor**less** /
fruit**less** / guilt**less** / hair**less** / harm**less** / heart**less** / help**less** /
home**less** / hope**less** / job**less** / meaning**less** / merci**less** /
pain**less** / piti**less** / reck**less** / rest**less** / ruth**less** / self**less** /
sight**less** / sleep**less** / spot**less** / taste**less** / time**less** / tire**less** /
tooth**less** / tree**less** / use**less** / water**less** / worth**less**

******

-lessly
Used to form: adverbs

General meaning: in a particular way

Examples:

care**lessly** / fear**lessly** / hope**lessly** / merci**lessly** / reck**lessly** / rest**lessly** / thought**lessly**

******

-lessness

Used to form: nouns

General meaning: the state of

Examples:

care**lessness** / color**lessness** / defense**lessness** / flavor**lessness** / grace**lessness** / heart**lessness** / heed**lessness** / help**lessness** / life**lessness** / match**lessness** / merci**lessness** / piti**lessness** / reck**lessness** / rest**lessness** / ruth**lessness** / sight**lessness** / tact**lessness** / taste**lessness** / thought**lessness** / water**lessness** / worth**lessness**

******

-let

Used to form: nouns

General meaning: small; unimportant

Examples:

book**let** / pig**let** / star**let**

******

-ling

Used to form: nouns

General meaning: small; unimportant

Examples:

duck**ling** / fledg**ling** / hatch**ling**

******

-ly

Used to form: adjectives and adverbs

General meaning: having the characteristic of; in a particular way; at particular intervals

Examples:

absolute**ly** / accidental**ly** / according**ly** / accurate**ly** / active**ly** / actual**ly** / additional**ly** / adequate**ly** / admitted**ly** / alert**ly** / alternate**ly** / alternative**ly** / angri**ly** / annual**ly** / anxious**ly** / apparent**ly** / apprehensive**ly** / approving**ly** / approximate**ly** / arrogant**ly** /assured**ly** / astute**ly** / attentive**ly** / audacious**ly** / austere**ly** / automatical**ly** / awful**ly** / awkward**ly** / bad**ly** / bare**ly** / bashful**ly** / basical**ly** / beautiful**ly** / benevolent**ly** / bigshearted**ly** / bitter**ly** / blank**ly** / blind**ly** / blissful**ly** / blunt**ly** / bold**ly** / brash**ly** / brave**ly** / brazen**ly** / brief**ly** / bright**ly** / broad**ly** / brutal**ly** / calm**ly** / candid**ly** / careful**ly** / caring**ly** / cautious**ly** / certain**ly** / cheap**ly** / cheeki**ly** / cheerful**ly** / chief**ly** / clear**ly** / clever**ly** / close**ly** / clumsi**ly** / cold**ly** / comfortab**ly** / common**ly** / comparative**ly** / competent**ly** / complete**ly** / concurrent**ly** / confident**ly** / consequent**ly** / considerate**ly** / constant**ly** / contented**ly** / continuous**ly** / converse**ly** / correct**ly** / corresponding**ly** / courageous**ly** / crazi**ly** / crude**ly** / cruel**ly** / cunning**ly** / curious**ly** / current**ly** / curt**ly** / customari**ly** / dangerous**ly** / daring**ly** / dazzling**ly** / decided**ly** / deep**ly** /

defectively / defiantly / definitely / deliberately / delicately / desperately / differently / diligently / directly / dishonestly / distinctively / doubtfully / dramatically / eagerly / earnestly / easily / effectively / efficiently / elegantly / eloquently / eminently / emotionally / enormously / entirely / enviously / equally / evenly / eventually / evidently / exactly / exceedingly / exclusively / expertly / explicitly / extensively / extravagantly / extremely / faintly / fairly / faithfully / fatally / ferociously / fiercely / finally / finely / firmly / fittingly / flagrantly / flamboyantly / fondly / foolishly / formally / formerly / fortuitously / fortunately / frankly / frantically / freely / frequently / freshly / fruitfully / fully / fundamentally / furiously / generally / generously / gently / genuinely / giftedly / gladly / gleefully / gracefully / gradually / gratefully / gravely / greatly / greedily / gruffly / habitually / happily / hardly / harshly / hastily / hazily / heatedly / heavily / hesitantly / highly / honestly / hopefully / horribly / hugely / hugely / humbly / hungrily / ideally / identically / illegally / immediately / impatiently / importantly / impressively / imprudently / increasingly / independently / indirectly / ineptly / inevitably / innocently / insolently / instantly / intensely / intently / jointly / justly / keenly / kindly / largely / lawfully / lazily / legally / lightly / lively / locally / lonely / loosely / loudly / lovingly / luckily / madly / mainly / marginally / meaningfully / mentally / merrily / mightily / mildly / mischievously / moderately / modestly / morally / mortally / munificently / mutely /

mysteriously / naturally / nearly / neatly / necessarily /
negligently / nervously / newly / nicely / noisily / normally /
obediently / obviously / occasionally / oddly / offensively /
openly / ordinarily / originally / painfully / particularly / partly /
passionately / patiently / perfectly / permanently / persistently /
personally / physically / piercingly / plainly / playfully /
pleasantly / pleasingly / pluckily / politely / politically / poorly /
positively / possibly / practically / precisely / presumably /
previously / primarily / principally / privately / probably /
prominently / promptly / properly / proudly / publicly /
punctually / purely / purposely / quickly / quietly / radiantly /
rapidly / rarely / readily / really / reasonably / recently /
regularly / relatively / reluctantly / remarkably / repeatedly /
resolutely / righteously / rightly / riskily / roughly / rudely /
sadly / safely / secretly / securely / selfishly / sensibly /
separately / serenely / seriously / severely / sharply / shiningly
/ shrewdly / shyly / sickly / significantly / silently / similarly /
simply / sincerely / skeptically / slickly / slightly / slowly /
smoothly / smugly / softly / solemnly / specifically / speedily /
steeply / sternly / stiffly / strangely / strictly / stridently /
strongly / stubbornly / stupidly / subsequently / successfully /
suddenly / sufficiently / superbly / surely / surprisingly /
suspiciously / sweetly / swiftly / teasingly / temporarily /
tenderly / tensely / terribly / thankfully / thickly / thoroughly /
thoughtfully / tightly / timidly / tiredly / tolerantly / totally /
traditionally / truly / typically / ultimately / understandingly /

undoubtedly / unexpectedly / unfairly / unfortunately /
uniformly / uniquely / unsteadily / unusually / unwillingly /
usually / vaguely / valiantly / vibrantly / violently / virtually /
vividly / weekly / widely / wildly / willingly / wisely / worriedly /
wrongly

Prefixes and Suffixes -- M

ENGLISH PREFIXES – M

mis-

Used to form: verbs and nouns

General meaning: bad or wrong

Examples:

misadventure / **mis**aligned / **mis**anthrope / **mis**application / **mis**apply / **mis**apprehension / **mis**appropriate / **mis**behave / **mis**behavior / **mis**calculate / **mis**cast / **mis**chance / **mis**conceive / **mis**conception / **mis**conduct / **mis**construction / **mis**count / **mis**diagnose / **mis**dial / **mis**direct / **mis**fire / **mis**fit / **mis**fortune / **mis**govern / **mis**guided / **mis**handle / **mis**hear / **mis**hit / **mis**inform / **mis**interpret / **mis**judge / **mis**lay / **mis**manage / **mis**match / **mis**name / **mis**place / **mis**print / **mis**pronounce / **mis**quote / **mis**read / **mis**report / **mis**represent / **mis**rule / **mis**spell / **mis**step / **mis**treat / **mis**trial / **mis**trust / **mis**understand / **mis**use

******

ENGLISH SUFFIXES – M

-ment

Used to form: nouns

General meaning: the action or result of

Examples:

ail**ment** / bombard**ment** / detri**ment** / develop**ment** /
disable**ment** / disinvest**ment** / enhance**ment** / enjoy**ment** /
enlarge**ment** / enrich**ment** / improve**ment** / merri**ment**

******

-mental

Used to form: adjectives

General meaning: having the characteristic of

Examples:

govern**mental** / judg**mental** / regi**mental**

******

-most

Used to form: adjectives

General meaning: the furthest

Examples:

in**most** / southern**most** / top**most** / up**most** / upper**most**

Prefixes and Suffixes -- N

ENGLISH PREFIXES – N

non-

Used to form: adjectives, adverbs and nouns

General meaning: not

Examples:

nonagenarian / **non**aggression / **non**alcoholic / **non**aligned / **non**appearance / **non**attendance / **non**chalant / **non**citizen / **non**combatant / **non**committal / **non**competitive / **non**compliance / **non**conforming / **non**conformist / **non**conformity / **non**controversial / **non**cooperation / **non**custodial / **non**dairy / **non**descript / **non**-distant / **non**-enforcement / **non**entity / **non**essential / **non**event / **non**executive / **non**existent / **non**fiction / **non**finite / **non**flammable / **non**-fulfillment / **non**human / **non**intervention / **non**invasive / **non**issue / **non**linear / **non**malignant / **non**native / **non**negotiable / **non**observance / **non**partisan / **non**payment / **non**person / **non**plussed / **non**-potable / **non**prescription / **non**professional / **non**profit / **non**proliferation / **non**proprietary / **non**refundable / **non**renewable / **non**resident / **non**returnable / **non**scientific / **non**sense / **non**-serious / **non**-settlement / **non**-silver / **non**slip / **non**smoker / **non**specific / **non**standard / **non**starter / **non**-state / **non**stick / **non**stop / **non**union / **non**verbal / **non**violence / **non**white

******

ENGLISH SUFFIXES – N

-ness

Used to form: nouns

General meaning: the characteristic or state of

Examples:

acute**ness** / aggressive**ness** / alert**ness** / appropriate**ness** / apt**ness** / arid**ness** / atrocious**ness** / attractive**ness** / awful**ness** / awkward**ness** / bad**ness** / baggi**ness** / bald**ness** / bare**ness** / bashful**ness** / bland**ness** / bleak**ness** / blind**ness** / bold**ness** / boring**ness** / brash**ness** / brazen**ness** / bright**ness** / bumpi**ness** / callous**ness** / calm**ness** / careful**ness** / cheap**ness** / cheerful**ness** / cheeri**ness** / childish**ness** / chilli**ness** / clammi**ness** / clever**ness** / close**ness** / cloudi**ness** / clumsi**ness** / coarse**ness** / cold**ness** / common**ness** / considerate**ness** / correct**ness** / corrupt**ness** / courteous**ness** / covetous**ness** / coy**ness** / crooked**ness** / crude**ness** / cumbersome**ness** / dainti**ness** / damp**ness** / dark**ness** / decisive**ness** / deft**ness** / devout**ness** / dim**ness** / dire**ness** / disgusting**ness** / distinctive**ness** / dizzi**ness** / drafti**ness** / dreari**ness** / droopi**ness** / dry**ness** / dull**ness** / duski**ness** / eager**ness** / earnest**ness** / edgi**ness** / empti**ness** / evasive**ness** / evenhanded**ness** / evil**ness** / exact**ness** / exclusive**ness** / exquisite**ness** / facile**ness** / faint**ness** / fair**ness** / faithful**ness** / fastidious**ness** / fast**ness** / fearful**ness** / ferocious**ness** / fierce**ness** / fine**ness** / firm**ness** / fit**ness** / flabbi**ness** / flat**ness** / fleet**ness** / fleshi**ness** / floppi**ness** / foggi**ness** / foolish**ness** / forceful**ness** / foul**ness** / fresh**ness** / friendli**ness** / frosti**ness** / game**ness** / gaudi**ness** / gawki**ness** /

gentle**ness** / genuine**ness** / ghastli**ness** / giddi**ness** / glad**ness** / glitzi**ness** / godli**ness** / good**ness** / gracious**ness** / great**ness** / greedi**ness** / grisli**ness** / gruesome**ness** / happi**ness** / hard**ness** / hasti**ness** / hazi**ness** / hefti**ness** / hideous**ness** / holi**ness** / honorable**ness** / horrendous**ness** / huge**ness** / ici**ness** / ill**ness** / impassive**ness** / impolite**ness** / impulsive**ness** / incorrect**ness** / indecisive**ness** / indecorous**ness** / industrious**ness** / inept**ness** / inert**ness** / jagged**ness** / jitteri**ness** / joyful**ness** / judicious**ness** / keen**ness** / kindhearted**ness** / kind**ness** / late**ness** / lightheaded**ness** / like**ness** / limber**ness** / limp**ness** / lithe**ness** / loose**ness** / loud**ness** / loutish**ness** / ludicrous**ness** / lumpi**ness** / lurid**ness** / mad**ness** / mean**ness** / meticulous**ness** / mild**ness** / miserli**ness** / misti**ness** / moist**ness** / moldi**ness** / mucki**ness** / muddi**ness** / narrow**ness** / nasti**ness** / neat**ness** / new**ness** / nice**ness** / normal**ness** / offensive**ness** / open**ness** / oppressive**ness** / ordinari**ness** / outlandish**ness** / outrageous**ness** / / parched**ness** / parsimonious**ness** / patchi**ness** / peaceful**ness** / pious**ness** / placid**ness** / plain**ness** / pleasant**ness** / plump**ness** / polite**ness** / praiseworthi**ness** / precarious**ness** / prepared**ness** / primitive**ness** / prompt**ness** / quick**ness** / quiet**ness** / rapid**ness** / rare**ness** / rash**ness** / raw**ness** / readi**ness** / real**ness** / reasonable**ness** / religious**ness** / repulsive**ness** / resolute**ness** / responsive**ness** / restive**ness** / revolting**ness** / ridiculous**ness** / righteous**ness** / robust**ness** / rough**ness** / rude**ness** / rugged**ness** / / sad**ness** / saggi**ness** / saintli**ness** / same**ness** / scrupulous**ness** / / selective**ness** / selfish**ness** / sensible**ness** / serious**ness** / shaki**ness** / sharp**ness** / shoddi**ness** / showi**ness** / shrewd**ness** / shy**ness** / sick**ness** / silli**ness** / slack**ness** / slender**ness** / slight**ness** / slim**ness** / slipperi**ness** / sloppi**ness** / slothful**ness** /

slow**ness** / smooth**ness** / soft**ness** / soggi**ness** / speedi**ness** /
spiteful**ness** / stale**ness** / stanch**ness** / stiff**ness** / still**ness** /
stingi**ness** / stout**ness** / strict**ness** / stubborn**ness** / stylish**ness** /
sweati**ness** / swift**ness** / tacki**ness** / tame**ness** / tardi**ness** /
taut**ness** / tawdri**ness** / tedious**ness** / tender**ness** / tense**ness** /
thick**ness** / thin**ness** / thorough**ness** / thoughtful**ness** /
tightfisted**ness** / tight**ness** / tiresome**ness** / trite**ness** / true**ness** /
trustworthi**ness** / truthful**ness** / ugli**ness** / uncertain**ness** /
unclean**ness** / uncouth**ness** / uneasi**ness** / uneven**ness** /
ungainli**ness** / unhappi**ness** / unkind**ness** / unpleasant**ness** /
unreasonable**ness** / unresponsive**ness** / unscrupulous**ness** /
unseemli**ness** / unsightli**ness** / unsteadi**ness** / unwieldi**ness** /
upright**ness** / vague**ness** / vast**ness** / vivid**ness** / wari**ness** /
watchful**ness** / weak**ness** / weari**ness** / weighti**ness** / wet**ness** /
wholehearted**ness** / wicked**ness** / wintri**ness** / woozi**ness** /
worthi**ness** / wretched**ness**

Prefixes and Suffixes -- O

ENGLISH PREFIXES – O

off-

Used to form: nouns, adjectives, verbs and adverbs

General meaning: not on; away

Examples:

off-screen / **off**-season / **off**-year / **off**-air / **off**-duty / **off**-key / **off**-limits / **off**-line / **off**-peak / **off**print / **off**-putting / **off**-road / **off**-sale / **off**-stage / **off**-street

******

oft-

Used to form: adjectives

General meaning: over and over again; frequently

Examples:

oft-quoted / **oft**-repeated

******

out-

Used to form: adjectives, nouns and verbs

General meaning: away from; better, longer, etc; outside

Examples:

outgoing / **out**grow / **out**growth / **out**gun / **out**last / **out**law / **out**live / **out**lying / **out**moded / **out**number / **out**patient / **out**perform / **out**play / **out**point / **out**rank / **out**run / **out**sell /

outshine / **out**size / **out**stretched / **out**strip / **out**vote / **out**weigh / **out**wit

******

over-

Used to form: nouns, verbs, adjectives and adverbs

General meaning: additional; beyond; too much; totally; upper; outer

Examples:

overachieve / **over**act / **over**age / **over**anxious / **over**balance / **over**blown / **over**book / **over**burden / **over**cast / **over**charge / **over**coat / **over**compensate / **over**confident / **over**cook / **over**critical / **over**crowded / **over**developed / **over**do / **over**draw / **over**eat / **over**emphasis / **over**estimate / **over**excited / **over**expose / **over**extended / **over**feed / **over**fishing / **over**flow / **over**generous / **over**graze / **over**grown / **over**growth / **over**hang / **over**hasty / **over**head / **over**heat / **over**indulged / **over**inflated / **over**joyed / **over**kill / **over**load / **over**manned / **over**pay / **over**populated / **over**priced / **over**produce / **over**production / **over**protective / **over**qualified / **over**rate / **over**react / **over**sell / **over**sensitive / **over**sized / **over**sleep / **over**spend / **over**staffed / **over**stay / **over**step / **over**subscribed / **over**tax / **over**time / **over**tired / **over**use / **over**value / **over**weight

******

ENGLISH SUFFIXES – O

-oid

Used to form: adjectives and nouns

General meaning: similar to

Examples:

human**oid** / rhomb**oid**

******

-or

Used to form: nouns

General meaning: a particular type of person or thing

Example:

act**or** / doct**or** / instigat**or** / invent**or** / jur**or** / originat**or**

******

-ory

Used to form: adjectives and nouns

General meaning: involving a particular action; a place for

Examples:

derogat**ory** / explanat**ory** / observat**ory**

******

-ous

Used to form: adjectives

General meaning: having the characteristic or nature of

Examples:

envi**ous** / malici**ous** / pi**ous** / precipit**ous** / religi**ous** / righte**ous** / venomo**us** / virtu**ous**

******

-ously

Used to form: adverbs

General meaning: in a particular way

Examples:

anx**iously** / audac**iously** / chivalr**ously** / conscient**iously** /
courage**ously** / courte**ously** / danger**ously** / fam**ously** /
gener**ously** / glor**iously** / hazard**ously** / industr**iously** /
judic**iously** / lumin**ously** / meticul**ously** / nerv**ously** / notor**iously**
/ ostentat**iously** / peril**ously** / pomp**ously** / ponder**ously** /
portent**ously** / precar**iously** / pretent**iously** / rauc**ously** /
rigor**ously** / scrupul**ously** / ser**iously** / treacher**ously**

******

-ousness

Used to form: nouns

General meaning: the state of

Examples:

capac**iousness** / gener**ousness** / malic**iousness** / pi**ousness** /
relig**iousness** / righte**ousness** / spac**iousness** / venom**ousness** /
vic**iousness** / virtu**ousness**

Prefixes and Suffixes -- P and Q

ENGLISH PREFIXES – P

para-

Used to form: adjectives, nouns

General meaning: beyond; partially

Examples:

paragliding / **para**medic / **para**military / **para**normal

******

post-

Used to form: adjectives, nouns, verbs

General meaning: after

Examples:

postdoctoral / **post**-examination / **post**graduate / **post**-Impressionist / **post**natal / **post**paid / **post**-production / **post**script / **post**-war

******

pre-

Used to form: adjectives, nouns, verbs

General meaning: before

Examples:

prearrange / **pre**-birth / **pre**-book / **pre**cancerous / **pre**caution / **pre**conceived / **pre**cooked / **pre**cut / **pre**dawn / **pre**exist / **pre**fabricate / **pre**heat / **pre**historic / **pre**industrial / **pre**judge / **pre**marital / **pre**mature / **pre**medication / **pre**occupied / **pre**-

owned / **pre**-packed / **pre**paid / **pre**qualifying / **pre**school / **pre**select / **pre**-stamped **/ pre**test / **pre**view / **pre**war / **pre**wash

******

pro-

Used to form: adjectives

General meaning: in favor of; supporting

Examples:

proactive / **pro**-democracy / **pro-**feminist / **pro-**liberal

******

ENGLISH SUFFIXES – P

-path

Used to form: noun

General meaning: relating to illness

Examples:

homoeo**path** / psycho**path**

Prefixes and Suffixes -- R

ENGLISH PREFIXES – R

re-

Used to form: adjectives, adverbs, nouns and verbs

Meaning: once more; again

Examples:

reabsorb / reaccept / reacquire / reactivate / readapt / readdress / readjust / readmit / readopt / re-advertise / reaffirm / reappear / reapply / reappoint / reappraise / rearrange / reassemble / reassert / reassess / reassign / reassure / reattach / rebirth / reborn / rebrand / rebroadcast / rebuild / recalculate / recall / recapture / recharge / recheck / reclaim / recollect / recombine / reconfigure / reconfirm / reconnect / reconsider / reconstitute / reconstruct / reconvene / reconvert / recreate / redecorate / redefine / redeliver / redeploy / redeposit / redesign / redevelop / redial / redirect / rediscover / redistribute / redraft / redraw / re-educate / reelect / re-emerge / reemploy / re-enact / reengage / re-enter / re-entry / reestablish / re-evaluate / re-examine / refasten / refigure / refill / reforestation / regain / regenerate / regroup / rehear / reheat / rehire / reincarnation / reintroduce / reinvent / reinvest / reinvestigate / reissue / rejoin / reload / relocate / relook / rematch / remix / rename / renew / reopen / reorder / reorient / repack / repackage / repay / replant / replay / re-present / repress / reprint / reprocess / reproduce / republish / rerecord / reregister / rerelease / reroll / rerun / reseal / reselect / resell / resettle / reshape / reshow / restart / resupply

/ **re**test / **re**transform / **re**translate / **re**trial / **re**tune / **re**type /

reunify / **re**unite / **re**usable / **re**use / **re**vote / **re**weave / **re**weigh /

reword / **re**work / **re**write

******

retro-

Used to form: adjectives, adverbs, nouns

Meaning: back or backwards

Examples:

retrograde / **retro**gressive / **retro**spective

******

ENGLISH SUFFIXES – R

-ry

Used to form: nouns

General meaning: the art, characteristic, practice or state of

Examples:

legenda**ry** / rival**ry**

Prefixes and Suffixes -- S

ENGLISH PREFIXES – S

semi-

Used to form: adjectives and nouns

General meaning: half; partly

Examples:

semi-arid / **semi**-automatic / **semi**-circle / **semi**circular / **semi**-conductor / s**emi**-darkness **/** **semi**-detached / **semi**-final / **semi**-organic / **semi**-precious / **semi**-prepared / **semi**-professional / **semi**-skilled / **semi**-skimmed / **semi**-stitched

******

sub-

Used to form: adjectives, nouns and verbs

General meaning: beneath; under; a part of

Examples

sub-aqua / **sub**atomic / **sub**committee / **sub**conscious / **sub**continent / **sub**contract / **sub**culture / **sub**directory / **sub**divide / **sub**division / **sub**editor / **sub**group / **sub**heading / **sub**human / **sub**marine / **sub**normal / **sub**section / **sub**set / **sub**soil / **sub**standard / **sub**tropical / **sub**urban / **sub**way / **sub**-zero

******

ENGLISH SUFFIXES – S

-s

Used to form: nouns (addition to nouns)

General meaning: belonging to

boy**'s** dress / men**'s** wear / bird**s'** nest / student**s'** books

******

-ship

Used to form: nouns

General meaning: the characteristic, state, status or office of; ability as; the group of

Examples:

citizen**ship** / friend**ship** / leader**ship** / member**ship** / musician**ship** / owner**ship** / professor**ship** / relation**ship**

******

-sion

Used to form: nouns

General meaning: the action or state of

Examples:

admis**sion** / colli**sion** / conclu**sion** / confes**sion** / confu**sion** / corro**sion** / deci**sion** / divi**sion** / ero**sion** / expres**sion** / repul**sion** / revi**sion**

******

-some

Used to form: adjectives and nouns

General meaning: likely to; a type of group

Examples:

fear**some** / four**some** / quarrel**some**

******

-ster

Used to form: nouns

General meaning: a person with a particular characteristic

Examples:

gang**ster** / mob**ster** / mon**ster** / young**ster**

Prefixes and Suffixes -- T

ENGLISH PREFIXES – T

trans-

Used to form: adjectives and verbs

General meaning: across; beyond; into another place or condition

Examples:

transatlantic / **trans**continental / **trans**cribe / **trans**form / **trans**genic / **trans**gress / **trans**lucent / **trans**migration / **trans**national / **trans**plant / **trans**port

******

ENGLISH SUFFIXES – T

-th

Used to form: nouns

General meaning: the characteristic or process of

Examples:

grow**th** / heal**th** / leng**th** / warm**th** / wid**th** / you**th**

Used to form: ordinal numbers

Examples:

fif**th** / fourteen**th** / hundred**th**

Prefixes and Suffixes -- U

ENGLISH PREFIXES – U

ultra-
Used to form: adjectives and nouns
General meaning: extremely; beyond a particular limit
Examples:
ultra-accurate / **ultra-**bright / **ultra-**cheap / **ultra-**cold / **ultra-**conservative / **ultra-**efficient / **ultra-**fast / **ultra-**high / **ultra-**intelligent / **ultra-**light / **ultra-**likeable / **ultra-**long / **ultra-**loose / **ultra-**low / **ultra-**luxurious / **ultra-**luxury / **ultra**marine / **ultra-**nationalist / **ultra-**orthodox / **ultra-**plush / **ultra-**precision / **ultra-**private / **ultra-**processed / **ultra-**productive / **ultra-**rich / **ultra-**rugged / **ultra-**secure / **ultra-**sensitive / **ultra-**short / **ultra-**slow / **ultra-**soft / **ultra**sonic / **ultra-**successful / **ultra-**thin / **ultra-**trim / **ultra-**violent / **ultra**violet / **ultra-**wealthy / **ultra-**wide

******

un-
Used to form: adjectives, adverbs, nouns and verbs
General meaning: not; the opposite of
Examples:
unable / **un**announced / **un**answerable / **un**answered / **un**anticipated / **un**apologetic / **un**appealing / **un**appetizing / **un**appreciated / **un**approachable / **un**arguable / **un**armed / **un**ashamed / **un**asked / **un**assailable / **un**assigned / **un**assisted / **un**assuming / **un**attached / **un**attainable / **un**attended /

unattractive / unauthorized / unavailable / unavoidable / unaware / unbalance / unban / unbearable / unbeatable / unbeaten / unbefitting / unbelief / unbelievable / unbeliever / unbelieving / unbend / unbending / unbiased / unblemished / unblinking / unblock / unborn / unbounded / unbowed / unbreakable / unbridgeable / unbridled / unbroken / unbuckle / unburden / unbutton / uncaring / unceasing / uncensored / unceremonious / uncertain / unchallengeable / unchallenged / uncharacteristic / uncharitable / uncharted / uncivil / uncivilized / unclaimed / unclassified / unclean / unclear / uncluttered / uncoil / uncolored / uncombed / uncomfortable / uncommitted / uncommon / uncommunicative / uncompetitive / uncomplaining / uncompleted / uncomplicated / uncomplimentary / uncomprehending / uncompromising / unconcealed / unconcern / unconditional / unconfined / unconfirmed / uncongenial / unconnected / unconquerable / unconscionable / unconscious / unconsidered / unconstitutional / unconstrained / uncontaminated / uncontested / uncontrollable / uncontroversial / unconventional / unconvinced / uncooked / uncooperative / uncoordinated / uncork / uncorroborated / uncountable / uncouple / uncover / uncritical / uncrowned / uncultivated / uncultured / uncurl / uncut / undamaged / undated / undaunted / undecided / undeclared / undefeated / undefended / undefined / undeleted / undemanding / undemocratic / undemonstrative / undeniable / undeserved / undesirable / undetectable / undeveloped / undifferentiated / undignified / undiluted / undiminished / undisciplined / undiscovered / undisguised / undismayed / undistinguished / undisturbed / undivided / undo / uneatable / uneconomical / uneducated / unelected / unemotional / unemployable / unequal / unethical / uneven / uneventful / unexceptionable / unexpected /

unexpired / unexplained / unexploded / unexplored / unexpressed / unfaithful / unfamiliar / unfashionable / unfeasible / unfilled / unfinished / unfit / unflappable / unfocused / unfold / unforced / unforgettable / unforgivable / unformed / unfortunate / unfulfilled / unfurl / unglamorous / ungodly / ungovernable / ungracious / ungrammatical / ungrateful / unguarded / unhappy / unharmed / unhealthy / unheard / unheated / unhelpful / unholy / unhurried / unhurt / unhygienic / unidentifiable / unimaginable / unimpaired / unimpeachable / unimpeded / unimportant / unimpressed / uninformative / uninhabitable / uninjured / uninspired / uninstall / uninsurable / unintelligent / unintended / unintentional / uninterested / uninterrupted / uninvited / uninvolved / unjust / unjustifiable / unjustified / unkind / unknowable / unknown / unlace / unlawful / unlearn / unleash / unlicensed / unlike / unlimited / unlined / unlisted / unlit / unload / unlock / unloose / unlucky / unmade / unmanageable / unmanly / unmanned / unmarried / unmatched / unmemorable / unmindful / unmistakable / unmitigated / unmodified / unmotivated / unmoved / unnamed / unnatural / unnecessary / unnerve / unnoticed / unnumbered / unobjectionable / unobserved / unobtainable / unoccupied / unofficial / unopened / unopposed / unorganized / unpack / unpaid / unpardonable / unpatriotic / unplanned / unpleasant / unpolished / unpolluted / unpopular / unprecedented / unpredictable / unprejudiced / unpremeditated / unprepared / unpretentious / unprincipled / unprintable / unproblematic / unproductive / unprofessional / unprofitable / unprotected / unproven / unprovoked / unpunished / unqualified / unquenchable / unquestionable / unquiet / unravel / unread / unreal / unreasonable / unreasoning / unrecognizable / unregenerate / unregulated / unrelated / unreliable / unrelieved /

unremarkable / unrepeatable / unrepentant / unreported / unrepresentative / unreserved / unresolved / unresponsive / unrest / unrestrained / unrestricted / unrewarded / unroll / unrounded / unsafe / unsaid / unsatisfactory / unsatisfied / unscathed / unscientific / unscripted / unscrupulous / unseasonal / unseat / unseeded / unseen / unselfish / unsentimental / unserviceable / unsettle / unshaken / unshaven / unskilled / unsmiling / unsociable / unsold / unsolicited / unsolved / unsophisticated / unsorted / unspeakable / unspecified / unspectacular / unspoiled / unstable / unstated / unsteady / unstoppable / unstressed / unstructured / unsubscribe / unsubstantiated / unsuccessful / unsuitable / unsure / unsurprised / unsuspected / unsustainable / unsweetened / unsympathetic / unsystematic / untalented / untamed / untangle / untested / unthinking / untidy / untimely / untitled / untouchable / untrained / untreated / untried / untrue / untrustworthy / untruth / untutored / untypical / unusable / unused / unusual / unvarnished / unveil / unvoiced / unwanted / unwarranted / unwary / unwashed / unwelcome / unwell / unwilling / unwise / unwitting / unworkable / unworldly / unworried / unworthy / unwrap / unyielding

******

under-
Used to form: adjectives, nouns and verbs
General meaning: below; beneath; insufficient; lower
Examples:
underachieve / underbelly / underbid / underbrush / undercharge / underclass / undercook / undercover /

underdeveloped / underdone / underemployed / underestimate / underfed / underfoot / underfunded / undergraduate / undergrowth / underinsured / underlay / underline / undermanned / underneath / undernourished / underpaid / underpass / underperform / underprepared / underpriced / underprivileged / underrate / underrepresented / under-resourced / undersea / undersell / underside / undersized / under-slept / understaffed / understated / underutilized / undervalue / underwater / underweight

******

up-
Used to form: adjectives, nouns and verbs
General meaning: higher; upwards
Examples:
upfield / upgrade / uphill / upland / uplift / upsurge / upswell / upswing / uptick / upturned

******

ENGLISH SUFFIXES – U

-ure
Used to form: nouns
General meaning: the action, process or result of
Examples:
closure / conjecture / departure / disclosure / exposure / failure / measure

Prefixes and Suffixes -- V

ENGLISH PREFIXES – V

viv-
Used to form: adjectives and nouns

General meaning: living; lively

Examples:

vivace / **viv**acious / **viv**arium / **viv**iparous / **viv**isection

******

ENGLISH SUFFIXES – V

-vore
Used to form: nouns

General meaning: that eats the particular thing

Examples:

avi**vore** / carni**vore** / herbi**vore** / insecti**vore** / omni**vore** /
ovi**vore** / pisci**vore** / vermi**vore**

Prefixes and Suffixes -- W

ENGLISH SUFFIXES – W

-ward

Used to form: adjectives

General meaning: in a particular direction

Examples:

back**ward** / east**ward** / home**ward**

******

-ways

Used to form: adjectives and adverbs

General meaning: in a particular direction

Examples:

length**ways** / side**ways**

******

-wise

Used to form: adjectives and adverbs

General meaning: in a particular manner or direction; concerning

Examples:

business**wise** / clock**wise** / like**wise**

Prefixes and Suffixes -- XYZ

ENGLISH SUFFIXES – XYZ

-y

Used to form: adjectives and nouns

General meaning: having the action, characteristic or process of; showing affection

Examples:

beaky / beardy / beefy / bendy / bloody / brainy / brushy / bushy / buttery / cakey / carroty / catchy / cheeky / chewy / choosey / classy / cloudy / coaly / coasty / cookery / cottony / creamy / crispy / curly / downy / drafty / dreamy / dressy / dusty / earthy / faulty / feathery / filmy / fishy / flashy / fleshy / fruity / girly / gluey / goody / grainy / grassy / hairy / handy / hardy / hearty / hilly / holey / hooky / horny / inky / irony / jokey / jumpy / leafy / leathery / lefty / lemony / massy / meaty / messy / milky / moody / needy / peppery / picky / pinky / pitchy / pointy / powdery / punchy / pushy / rainy / righty / risky / rocky / roomy / ropey / rubbery / salty / sandy / scratchy / screwy / seedy / shadowy / showy / silky / silvery / sleepy / smelly / smiley / snowy / softy / soldiery / soupy / speedy / spidery / sporty / steamy / steely / sticky / stormy / stretchy / stripy / stuffy / sugary / sweaty / teary / toothy / touchy / trendy / watery / wealthy / weighty / whispery / whitey / windy / wintery / woody / wooly / wordy

-zoic

Used to form: adjective

General meaning: relating to animal life

Example:

Ceno**zoic** / Meso**zoic** / Paleo**zoic**

＊＊＊＊＊＊＊＊＊＊＊＊＊＊＊＊

About the Author

Manik Joshi, the author of this book was born on **Jan 26, 1979** at Ranikhet and is permanent resident of Haldwani, Kumaon zone of India. He is an Internet Marketer by profession. He is interested in domaining (business of buying and selling domain names), web designing (creating websites), and various online jobs (including 'self-publishing'). He is science graduate with ZBC (zoology, botany, and chemistry) subjects. He is also an MBA (with specialization in marketing). He has done three diploma courses in computer too. **ManikJoshi.com** is the personal website of the author.

Amazon Author Page of Manik Joshi:
https://www.amazon.com/author/manikjoshi

Email:
mail@manikjoshi.com

****

BIBLIOGRAPHY

'ENGLISH DAILY USE' TITLES BY MANIK JOSHI

01. How to Start a Sentence
02. English Interrogative Sentences
03. English Imperative Sentences
04. Negative Forms in English
05. Learn English Exclamations
06. English Causative Sentences
07. English Conditional Sentences
08. Creating Long Sentences in English
09. How to Use Numbers in Conversation
10. Making Comparisons in English
11. Examples of English Correlatives
12. Interchange of Active and Passive Voice
13. Repetition of Words
14. Remarks in English Language
15. Using Tenses in English
16. English Grammar- Am, Is, Are, Was, Were
17. English Grammar- Do, Does, Did
18. English Grammar- Have, Has, Had
19. English Grammar- Be and Have
20. English Modal Auxiliary Verbs
21. Direct and Indirect Speech
22. Get- Popular English Verb
23. Ending Sentences with Prepositions
24. Popular Sentences in English
25. Common English Sentences
26. Daily Use English Sentences
27. Speak English Sentences Everyday
28. Popular English Idioms and Phrases
29. Common English Phrases
30. Daily English- Important Notes

ALSO BY MANIK
Simple, Compound, Complex, & Compound-Complex Sentences

'ENGLISH WORD POWER' TITLES BY MANIK JOSHI

01. Dictionary of English Synonyms
02. Dictionary of English Antonyms
03. Homonyms, Homophones and Homographs
04. Dictionary of English Capitonyms
05. Dictionary of Prefixes and Suffixes
06. Dictionary of Combining Forms
07. Dictionary of Literary Words
08. Dictionary of Old-fashioned Words
09. Dictionary of Humorous Words
10. Compound Words in English
11. Dictionary of Informal Words
12. Dictionary of Category Words
13. Dictionary of One-word Substitution
14. Hypernyms and Hyponyms
15. Holonyms and Meronyms
16. Oronym Words in English
17. Dictionary of Root Words
18. Dictionary of English Idioms
19. Dictionary of Phrasal Verbs
20. Dictionary of Difficult Words

ALSO BY MANIK
List of 5000 Advanced English Words

∗∗∗∗∗∗∗∗∗∗∗∗∗∗∗∗

59229762R00052

Made in the USA
Lexington, KY
28 December 2016